T0322171

GREEN NOISE

GREEN NOISE

Jean Sprackland

CAPE POETRY

3 5 7 9 10 8 6 4 2

Jonathan Cape, an imprint of Vintage,
20 Vauxhall Bridge Road,
London SW1V 2SA

Jonathan Cape is part of the Penguin Random House group of companies
whose addresses can be found at global.penguinrandomhouse.com

Penguin
Random House
UK

First published by Jonathan Cape in 2018

penguin.co.uk/vintage

A CIP catalogue record for this book is available
from the British Library

ISBN 9781787330924

Typeset in 11/13 pt Bembo by Jouve (UK), Milton Keynes
Printed and bound by CPI Group (UK) Ltd, Croydon, CR0 4YY

Penguin Random House is committed to a sustainable future for
our business, our readers and our planet. This book is made
from Forest Stewardship Council® certified paper.

MIX
Paper | Supporting
responsible forestry
FSC
www.fsc.org
FSC® C018179

Was there
some moment
dividing
song from no song?

Denise Levertov

CONTENTS

APRIL

machine of spring with all your levers thrown to max
clouds in ripped clothes and sheep trailing afterbirth
where last week's buds sucked blue juice from the dusk
now the branch is swollen   priapic
cherry bling and hawthorn sex-bed smell
motorway hedgerows on thrust   electric rapefields

your levers are jammed and nothing can pull them back
not now   not frost   not squall
city gutters clogged with blossom
muddy ponds spuming with cannibal tadpoles
the long blinding days   your bashed clock
the violent small hours   magpie clacking at the robin's nest

and us lying open-eyed all night
breathing in the green noise of pollen
hearing the long bones of the trees stretch and crack
wondering   will you ever power down or is this it now
wondering   what can any death amongst us mean to you
and will we make it through to summer or is this it now

OAK APPLES

I. Gall wasp

She escaped from the convent
at the root of the oak
with only one idea in mind.
No need of a mate – she had everything
ready-packed inside her.

She was wingless, androgynous.
Her thorax and abdomen
were like polished mahogany.
Each antenna had fifteen segments
and each leg was sprung and clawed.

She traversed the rootscape
to the trunk, its rough slab
scarred with deep ravines,
climbed to where the branches
divide and divide again,

stepped smartly along those rafters,
inspecting the new leafbuds
swollen by early spring rain.
She made her choice,
drew out her fine needle,

eased it between the folded leaflets
to pierce the heart of the bud
and lay her white eggs.
Then she sealed the future
with a shot of venom

to swell and soften the tissues,
bed in the eggs till hatching time.
It was done. A gust of wind
snatched her from the branch,
weightless as blown grass.

But the winged generation
which would grow from those eggs
and drill their way out into the light –
how different they would be.
Airborne, of course, and sexual.

II. Eve

It must have been boredom. Hard to believe
she actually longed to taste one –
they were plain and meagre
and times were not exactly hard. Anyhow

she was pacing the garden,
swinging a stick, talking to herself
(more fun than listening to *him*)
and slashing at camphire and spikenard,

when she stopped under the oak
and saw it was hung with small fruits,
each tucked in tight to the branch,
green streaked with pink. She hesitated

then reached to pluck one,
cool and spongy to the touch.
Poor girl, how sickening
to bite into the wasp nursery

and get a mouthful of those
fat little ghosts in their nest. Well
it wouldn't be the last time
one of us took that kind of risk

and tasted nothing but bitterness.
Such spitting and retching, such grief.
The vessel smashed, the spell undone,
the larvae spilt and naked in the grass.

III. Apothecary's boy

Barefoot, ragged, snotty-nosed, he is out in the woods
on a November morning, when the last of the leaves have fallen
and the old galls are easy to spot in the bones of the branches.

They are brittle now, punctured by many exit wounds,
empty and weatherbeaten since the young wasps flew
and all the hungry invaders and colonisers came and went.

His job is to pick them, or gather them from the ground
where they lie spent in the leaf litter. If he's lucky
there might be a few beechnuts the pigs have missed

but he has to be quick, he mustn't go back empty-handed,
he has to break the galls to pieces, crush them in the mortar,
then mix the powder with water to draw out the tannin.

His master will do the rest, measuring, adding, stirring the pot
with a fig stick, until brown gives way to black:
a smooth, translucent, indelible ink, the favourite of scribes,

perfect for good law and bad law, statute, deed, decree,
for every map, census, peace treaty, declaration of war
in this boy's lifetime and for thirty generations to come,

though over the centuries it will corrode these important words,
burn its way through the parchment they are written on,
quietly eat them to dust in our vaults and archives:

chronicle, constitution, gospel, papal bull, and even
the old apothecary's own recipe: *To make hynke.*
Take gall & coporos or vitrial quartryn & gumme of eueryche . . .

IVY

I appeal this sentence –

the agony   think of it
to be wrenched   hacked
from these your shabby battlements

(long ago slipped and settled
pocked with faults and fissures)

where I   hurting no one
lactated a little pale glue
put down my holdfasts

surveyed for the thinnest of keyholes
tricked in my root-hair keys
made spiral locks of them

I am steel cable and shag
and green fists for flowers
I can burn the hands to blisters
I can choke the blood cell by cell

but was I not loved
by innkeepers   brides
butchers with knives to whet
travelling preachers with broken feet

have I not provided
brew of bruised leaves for the hangover
cap of woven stems for baldness
berries crushed in red wine
for the plague and the bloody flux

and see   even now
how I can stop you in your tracks
on this city street at dusk
with the sudden scent of honey   and jism

EXODUS

A dark expedition to fetch more logs
from where they're stacked in the lean-to
under a crippled roof of old felt.
The air barbed with frost and held breath.

Only one glove, and the shock
of bare hand on calloused bark,
furred and intimate with moss.
(Once there was candlesnuff fungus
like small white antlers in the gloom.)

Toss a few thudding into the basket,
hear the stack shift and settle. Good fuel
from the old ash which looked dead last spring.
Take it right back, said a neighbour, it might recover,
and new buds swelled between the wounds.

The night is moonless, watchful.
Up the steps with the creaking basket,
back to the hearth and throw on a log
which hisses and keens and oozes sap
and now in the firelight I see how it is,

how it always is: life scrambling out
from the rifts and crevices, life
too small to name, or too fast to be sure –
woodlouse or pillbug, spider, weevil,
click beetle, darkling beetle, millipede –

all running from their private rooms
and galleries and gardens, and away
over the street of hot tiles, an exodus
of everything that can, and the rest left burning.

IN THE CASTLE

What, then, are these three things of the thing?
Jacques Derrida

When I visited the castle and read about what had happened there –
a nobleman tricked into meeting to sort out some differences,
the guidebook was vague on what or why,
but he was in his nightclothes, had just finished his supper,
the girl who came to clear the table was in on it,
still she felt her throat ache as she watched him unfold the note,
his eyes brightening as he read it,
he was getting tired of all this aggravation,
there might after all be something to be said for a quiet life,
she thought of warning him, but no, impossible,
so she went on loading the silver tray, a family piece,
his grandmother had brought it from the old country,
it was engraved with peacocks,
under strange weeping trees which were dropping their fruit,
if you looked closely you could see some rotting on the ground,
there was even a crown of flies over it,
and he fussed about, re-tying his robe, pomading his hair,
the mirror he used was the one I was looking into now,
scratched and blown like a winter pond thawed and refrozen,
and all the time she knew they were here,
whispering in the kitchen,
she fingered the key in her apron pocket,
and they would take the back stairs, enter without knocking,
one leading the way with a bow then stepping aside,
to let the next through with his long knife,
and it was going dark in the knot garden,
and the tea-room was closing,
they were stacking the chairs and cashing up the till,

and everything was turning away from the light,
taking this room with it,
the old duke, and those who wanted him dead,
the mirror, the girl with the key, the smoky fire in the grate,
the silver fruit devoured by flies the only token of summer —
then I thought about the lovely words dusk and November,
and all the other words,
stacked hard against the door as if they could keep it shut.

THE LOST VILLAGES

THE LOST VILLAGE

I. A bend in the lane,

and there it is:
sheer limestone,
white altarpiece
erupting from the sunlit field

ash tree manifest above
cave beneath
and on a shelf of white rock
a ewe and her lamb –

Our Lady of the Field
still watchful
as if the bloody centuries
meant nothing

and all around
the scattered ruins

II. *The fourth house*

When it comes to the question of where you belong
don't look to the sky, as you learned in childhood,
for isn't it proven that the sky is not in fact blue,
that its acres are vast and mostly sown with nothing?

The planets themselves are dumb and geriatric,
all worked-out mines and dry lakebeds. No,
this is a question for ground, not sky.
And when you take a handful of earth from our village,

or the place where they say our village was,
you take a little of the wisdom of our dead.
All those other things – residue, runoff, fallout –
are trivial compared with that wisdom.

Ask nothing yet. The dead give many answers
to the same question. Did you ever
crouch in the village square with your friends,
toss the metal jacks and let them fall anyhow?

Querent, you're taller now. Throw your handful of earth
high enough for the breeze to shuffle it,
and watch it fall where it will. Now let's crouch together
where the square might have been and read the answer.

III. The ghosts

The ghosts are back, tracing the lines
of buried toft and twitchel, scuffing up
bone and flint, bits of Anglo-Saxon brooch.
They have forgotten how it ended

but they remember the old names.
Drakelow: *dragon's mound.*
Wychnor: *bank of the Hwicci people.*
Hungry Bentley: *poor clearing in the cropped grass.*

Like ashes raked from the furnace,
scattered and washed between earth and stones,
the ghosts long to return to source,
but everything is so temporary:

the field a ley, the stream a leat.
All the houses have new faces,
the old inn is chipboard and ragwort.
The ghosts come scraighting along the lanes

to Tamhorn, Cold Eaton, Hoon,
each name a drawer pulled and slammed
for something no longer kept there.
They can't remember how it ended

but they can never forget the smell:
corn rotting in the flooded field,
smouldering of piled fleece
or black gangrene in the hands and feet.

IV. Common knowledge

Everyone knew how butter was made.
They had all seen milk brought to the dairy,
bluish and steaming, flecked with straw,
knew you had to strain it through muslin,
crank the churn till your hand blistered,
knew the changing sound it made
passing through its several stations:
thickening then separating,
coming together and coming apart.
They knew the reek of sweat and ripeness,
the pouring, rinsing, pressing, patting.

From everyday milk, lipping the pail
as the dairymaid lugged it in from the field
to fat pound of gold on the slab:
a miracle everyone understood.
Only the cow knew nothing of it
as the silkmoth knows nothing of shantung
or the tree of this paper I'm writing on.
She went on chewing and pissing and swatting
flies with her tail, and dreamed of the girl
with the blistered hands kicking the gate
and trailing over the mud to meet her.

V. Alms

It happened here, under the flyover,
where the old crossroads used to be.
A girl, a cart, a stranger – that's all we know.

Back then there was a granite cross
and steps down to a well beneath.
You can still see a course of stones,
the depression where holy water collected
and money was washed clean of the plague.

Deep inside lived a captive demon
and if a traveller should break his journey here
and take water, but give no alms in return
the well would echo with laughter, they say,
and a *jubilation of chains*.

No one knows what happened to the girl,
or what happened to the stone cross.
Hacked to pieces and carried away,
stuck in a crypt, a garden, a ditch,
used to prop something up, or hold it down.

Hard to picture any of this, I know,
under the shuddering concrete
with its parings of lorry tyre,
smear of smashed headlight,
grey scurf of noise over everything.

The demon? I really couldn't say.
No one stops to kneel at the wellstones now.
No one swerves off onto the verge,
jumps out and scrambles down the bank
to drag a pocket and toss a groat
into the patch of moss and meadowsweet.

VI. Landfill

Bonetide and spurshift,
light the colour of dust,
everything lost

and only the weighbridge doing the reckoning,
only the aquifer keeping the inventory.

Once wedding gift, now ashdrift.
No receipts for the dead,
nothing to write in your ledger, scribe.

And do they come over the brow of the hill?
Do they come looking for it,
the thing they dream of
in the long nights underground?

It spreads, it spreads, on sometime
wheatfield and pasture, meadow and leasow,
neither is the battlefield exempt.

Sky wheeling over, streaked with cries.
Wind's teeth tearing at the clotted jelly.
Reek and deliquescence.
If they come, we never see them.

Spruetide and shitdrag,
rain the colour of rat:
plough all in together, ploughman.

But first
the slow procession of yellow machines
to turn over the relics
and to mourn.

VII. Everything looks like something else

Watercress, glimpsed under running water
in a chalk stream or scythed ditch

is easily confused with Fool's Watercress
(toothed leaves and a faint smell of carrot).

This in turn resembles Water Parsnip
(once grown for its sweet tuber)

which is hard to distinguish from Water Dropwort
(Children's Bane or Suicide Root).

Everyone knew you should harvest it
from the swift middle of the stream

not pull it up, roots and all,
from the shallows by the bank,

not take it home, as they say he did,
for his wife to cook with apple sauce,

for the three children to eat, then stagger
vomiting down the road for the doctor

who could only watch and shake his head.
People were so much hungrier then

and everything looks like something else.
No one gathers watercress here now

but kneel by the ditch and part the nettles
and you'll see it, or something like it.

VIII. Human things

In a quaggy place by the cut
where Thickbroome or Syerscote used to be,
one of the ghosts lies starved with cold
in an iron bath, three inches of rainwater.

Another, searching at Fraiforde
for cart-tracks on the old baulk,
has found instead a television,
flat out in the mud, and rimed with moss.
He stands and watches a while
as clouds and crows flicker over the screen.

Such long memories
these human things must have, he thinks.
The bath still full, the movies running.
They seem to love us don't they
in spite of everything.

IX. Solar field

The field is mirrors now, the sky can look at itself all day.
The people are done with ploughing, with woodcutting,
done with open-air preaching, witness, unlawful assembly.

No workers come here from warehouse or distribution centre.
No rebels gather at the stand of beech
in common cause against *incroaching tirants which would
grind our flesh upon the whetstone of poverty.*

The people are done with the harrow and done with the stook,
and done with coupling in the lee of the hedge.
The field is mirrors now, and if the hawk still ripples overhead

she sees first the muscular shock of the wings, and then
the scale of her empty precincts and palaces.

X. Where the farm was

The lake whips up froth
blows knots of it over the grass
fastens them to the barbed wire fence

But no   these are not froth   they're wool
ash-pale on rusty steel
a row of thin old beards   tugged by the wind
brindled with fog and smoke
spiked with seeds   bark   spider   leaf skeleton

The flock has bolted
all but a single ewe   barely more than a lamb
one my grandfather would have called a *theave*

She stands her ground
stares at me   or through me
pupil black as a slot in a gritstone wall

as I take a piece   rub it between my fingers
feel it greased and barbed   crimped and corkscrewed
feel it slip   and catch on itself
more rugged than it looks
the grist of hard livings   scraped from these hills

White froth races off the lake   lit   spectacular

but that slot of an eye
goes on watching me
perhaps with contempt   perhaps indifference

as I search this raw scrap of her
trying to fathom this
bit of field spun into fleece
getting nowhere   staining my hand
with sweat and oil and weather

Blinks shut   stares again

DANDELIONS

Pale lamps on waste ground
in the stillness after rain,

a reminder of the fine crystal
that used to be made here:

boys I knew from school
working the glass with diamond,
roughing and smoothing, making
their mitre, flute and thumbprint cuts.

Some lamps are blown and splintered,
some grazed by tiny slugs,

jet-black, glistening, each
light enough to be held by this
slight architecture, each enacting

the parable of the pondskater
borne by surface tension,
or the spider by its own silk:

the world somehow supporting
the weight of its griefs.

APHID FARM

Its acreage is small — a few new shoots
where the plum tree has put out leaves.
Turn one, already thickened with glair,
and see them crowding at the veins to feed,
mouths latched tight to draw off the sap.

Last month the farmer ants
drove the herd to these spring pastures
from the hatchery in their nest
where the eggs were kept all winter.

Now they graze peacefully
and the farmers move among them,
counting and checking and keeping watch,
sweating dope from the soles of their feet,
keeping the cattle stoned and docile.

Each one a green chit, small enough
to stick under a fingernail,
to be prised and flicked like snot.
If there's suffering, it's too faint to hear

though it is the job of one class of ant
to bite off the wings of the young,
and in a bad season, when the yield is poor,
it's sound husbandry
to slaughter a third of the stock for meat.

Gentleness too is beyond our hearing.
They use their antennae to stroke them stupid –
steady old girl, cush cush –
till they let down their milk:

this milk of paradise,
ambrosia, honeydew –
so abundant it runs from the leaf
and drips into the dust.

HELMHOLTZ RESONATOR

Late afternoon, and a trembling note
rises like tinnitus
through the traffic racket

silenced by passing sirens then rising again,
gaining strength, finding pitch,
tuning itself to a clear B flat.

Remember the first day of the holidays,
the long drive to the coast
in the old Cortina, with the roof-rack on?

Remember sitting on a sea wall
blowing across the top of an empty bottle?
Now run barefoot like a child into the street

where wind is throwing the blue ropes
lashed to the scaffolding on your neighbour's house,
skimming the mouths of the metal poles

and every mouth responds with song.

DEAR STREET

Dear street, you're all mixed up –
paved with crushed rowanberries
and shadows, though even

midwinter sun climbs high enough
to sit on the roofs, spilling its sherbet
into the road below,

and the phone booth has forgotten
everything, stripped and stinking
like the pillbox where we made dens.

Old street, you speak in the voices
I knew as a child: tyres on wet tarmac,
dog-bark, fox-bark. But also

that sawn-off talk on mobiles,
and always a powertool on the go,
always something being spliced or riven.

Your lamps know when to come on at night,
and curtains are drawn at every window
to keep the bad news from leaking out,

so when a plane sharks over
with its cargo of doubts
street, please still your trembling.

ON DEEP WATER

'Noise' – origin Middle English: from Old French,
from Latin nausea, *from Greek* nausia, *from* naus *'ship'*

The zero of it. The steep descent into nothing
as though the drowned landscape you feel
open up beneath you as you scull across the lake
is not beneath but inside you, and the boat
that gimcrack thing of fibreglass

in which you ride the everydays, dip and pull
between the baffling shores
smiling and waving: *this is me.*

But the dread of deep water. You ship the oars
and drift frail as a leaf over precipice and gorge
where so many adventurers have lost their way.

No ropes are long enough, you tell yourself,
to bring them back, crashing through the surface,
blue-faced, clawing for one more touch of the sun. So

in your faded skiff, only just seaworthy,
you slide over the void of yourself. Each day
one long trick at the helm, and sometimes
kneeling and gripping the side, sick with vertigo,
which is after all a kind of longing.

REMEMBERING

Then there's the black noise:

the not-quite-silence that can fill up
the forecourt of the redundant petrol station:
hardstanding split by thistles,
hinterland of half-bricks and goat-willow,
fuel pumps mute as witnesses, and still
that flammable smell, after all these years.

Childhood is an abridgement,
and we are made of such absences

though there is from time to time
a faint pulse, a dull glint in the rubble –
marble, bottle-top – something
rolled to the edge of the mind.

THE PERMANENT WAY

Where are they
the children who used to play here

squatting on the old trackbed
where the grey ballast is deciphered
into shades of blue and white?

It's just crushed granite of course
trucked by the ton from the nearest quarry

just magma, long cooled and hardened
hewn, spalled, put to work
shovelled by platelayer, raked by lengthman
to bear the load and the shock as it passes

but in summer
these stones were bleached and chalky
and we'd work our bare feet between them

feel their weight
find their darker undertones
learn how shallow the day's warmth is
how near and insistent the earth's chill

and we'd examine the oak sleepers
blackened by creosote, split by age
we knew that sleepers were cut from trees
were living once as we were now

and the greenish clips that fix the rails
and the rails dulled with rust
except for a line the wheels had polished silver

Then they began their scratchy song
and we scrambled away
up the embankment –

I want to climb there now, find us still lying
barefoot in the willowherb

Nothing left of that life
but the stones

Is it too late to feel my way back?
Crouching like a child
to touch these blue-and-white
offcuts of the past

Then the slam
the sucked-out street of air
time seized, shaken loose

PLUMS AND CUSTARD

Near the house where I was born was a wood,
deep as a dream, with a brook rushing through it
and a deathly waterfall you could cross in bare feet.
At the far edge there were sinking sands
and a fishing place called Roaring Rocks.

I was often lost on its tracks and clearings,
one with a bony tree where an owl stared,
another where I met a boy with no voice
who threw jumping jacks at squirrels
and let me try his Players No. 6.

I suppose that tree was felled long ago
and Roaring Rocks made still and fishless.
But surely the boy remembers those mushrooms
called plums and custard, that tasted of ditchwater.

DOGGY PADDLE

i.m. Robert Hawthorne Lockley

When he sprints down the beach in those navy shorts
he must have had since the year dot
I see how lean he is, I see
the long white scar on his right shin
where the empty coal truck crushed his leg
and his friend ran back to tell his mother:
Your Robert's been run over by a train.
He launches himself like a paper aeroplane
over a breaking wave, takes a few
brief splashing strokes, and then
the moment I'm waiting for, the same routine
on every family holiday, when
he treads water and yaps like a terrier.
I laugh, he laughs. He's such a good mimic.

Years later I'll learn that he hated swimming,
could not really swim at all. He
who is brave about jellyfish, doesn't mind seaweed.
Farm boy, poor boy,
living a hundred miles from the sea,
how would he ever have learned? So
does he undress in a sharp breeze
and put on those ancient shorts out of love?
Perhaps the joke is not only a joke, the game
more mine than ours. Too late to ask
and anyway not the kind of question
he would have understood. He scans the beach
for his clothes and paper and flask of tea.
I think I'll go in, he says. Meaning out.

SCIENCE

It wasn't knowledge we were after
when we plunged our hands into
a silty brainmass of frogspawn
and pulled out long drooling strings
to desiccate on the grass,

knelt coughing under the hedge
with matches and a damp mattress
watching smoke slink into the road
and over the neighbouring gardens,

or dammed the brook, testing all afternoon
with mud gouged from the bank
and sticks for the wattle-and-daub,
grit for structure, and riverweed for proofing.

What we really cared for, then as now,
was sensation – the fierce life of the body,
all the ways we could press it to the world.
When an uncle with no children of his own
came to visit, bringing a chemistry set,

it was seized and gutted,
fingers dipped in coloured crystals,
corrosive liquids sniffed and spilt,
only the instruction book left untouched

then quickly out to mate worms
or throw sticks at pigeons' nests,
leaving the scattered treasures, the ripped box
and its illustration of an enraptured boy
with a white coat and a rack of test-tubes.

I can't say which was more instructive:
stopping the watercourse, making it
pool and spread where it shouldn't,
or watching our work destroyed, the force released.
I liked to stay on when the others had gone

and guard the sooty mattress, the breached dam.
Crouching alone at the centre of everything,
under the hedge, with its museum of cobwebs,
or in the middle of the brook, where minnows
sleeked my bare legs as they ran between.

COAL AND COKE

They lived side by side in asbestos bunkers
where I would play, though I wasn't allowed.
One I loved for its deep, reflective gravity,
the other for its airy, roughcast charm.
One stained my hands with prehistoric soot,
the other was sharp enough to leave them clean.
One slabbed and weighty and impervious,
the other skittish, light as blown eggs.

During long compression in the deep earth of childhood
I spent whole afternoons there, alone
with the smell of the coke, clean as white sugar,
and the treacly otherness of the coal. Impossible
to choose, I thought, as I heard my father whistling
on his way to fill the scuttle and to find me.

CRYSTALLOGRAPHY

My brother was growing crystals in vinegar,
in the old lean-to we called the verandah.
I thought these boughs and blooms were forged
in the crucible of my brother's attention,
I thought them an outpost of his cleverness.

Close-up they were bristly in texture,
like iron filings clumped on a magnet.
And the colours unearthly, absolute.
He said they were not plants, but they looked so
mossy and heliotropic, I imagined them
clipped and trained like our neighbours' hedge.

I recall him now, bent to his task –
he was growing so tall these days –
out there among the woodlice
and the green shelves split by sunlight,
checking the levels, inspecting the accretions.
I watched from a distance, I would avoid that place

and even now the smell of white vinegar
troubles me with thoughts of unnatural growth
and the strong life of the inert.
I, who used to follow him everywhere,
watching through glass as he went before breakfast
to tour his strange gardens, to see
how his life had changed while he slept.

DUMB ANIMALS

In particular the school guinea pig
which broke free once or twice a term
and sought asylum under the PE shed.
Then a child would be sent with a key
to fetch out hockey sticks, and we'd kneel
and try to hook him out from his hiding place.

I remember the feel of the rubbery grip,
the unravelling threads, red and white,
the stick skived and chipped
from all the bully-off it had seen.
How desperately I longed to be the one
to bring him out into the light.

But even with the shed surrounded,
kids on all four sides with their small shoulders
pressed to the concrete slabs and arms stretched
as far as they would reach, I reckoned
there was a cool dark region in the centre
which was beyond us, and if only he could
find his way there he'd be safe.

Still I swung and scraped my stick,
wretched with desire and dread,
until he hurtled screaming into the hands
of some quick girl who bore him in like a prize
to be caged and pacified with dandelion leaves.

THREE IDYLLS

Censorship
Seeing the grey abbreviated bodies of military aircraft at the edge of a field, I remember at once the dismantled flies in the corner of the playground. I would sneak back when the committee had gone, to see if the engines had stopped and to inspect the exhausted machinery. I didn't dare touch, but when I held my finger close I could feel the molecules of air still stirring faintly with warmth. As for the wings, who knows what happened to them? The provocative wings! Like scandalous scraps of film they were excised, and taken as trophies or lost to the wind.

Sent to Coventry
The official notice of exile was written on a page torn from a maths book. I folded it neatly into my blazer pocket. There were simultaneous equations on the other side. For the first few days it was hard to remember: remnants of speech would spill from my mouth, and were walked underfoot by the crowd. I took out the paper when no one was looking. I licked my lips and licked them till they bled. I stared at the equations, but they weren't part of it.

'Wicksteed of Kettering'
Back at the playground, the committee arrived on bikes. First the necessary evictions, then they seized the swings. They began throwing them over the top of the frame and catching them. They worked in silence, throwing and catching, throwing and catching. The metal chains grew shorter, they juddered and bunched into knots, and soon the swings were cancelled. How clean and spacious the frame was now. They stood and smoked, flicking ash into the pits of dust where feet had scuffed the summer grass. I crawled out of the hedge and stood underneath, looking up at the red plastic seats, and I noticed that each one was stamped with the revolutionary slogan.

RESISTANCE

One day in 1980 –
perhaps the sweltering June day I sat my General Studies A-Level
and read the question about the USSR
and whether it could be expected to survive the age of
    globalisation
and sat for forty-five minutes
scraping the red-and-black striped paint off my pencil
(Staedtler, Made in Germany, Art. Nr. 110-HB) –

two Brothers deep in the forest near Ruusmäe
took the last pair of binoculars and broke it in half with a stone
and went their separate ways taking one piece each.

RED HORSES

Red horses in a forest, moving stiffly
as if they have not moved in a long time,

as if they are too red to move freely
in this green world,

or have escaped here
from some indoor shelf or mantelpiece

having heard about the felling and the burning,
felt the ache in their big sinewy hearts,

had to get back here
and see it before it's too late.

It's more than a place, says one of them,
it's in the blood, makes me the horse I am.

The forest is calling them home, they agree,
it's their heritage, their birthright,

no matter that they are red, bright red,
and seem to be made of wood.

They come creaking along the old tracks
and birds clatter away to the high branches.

They stand uncertainly in a clearing
like extravagant flowers blooming in the wrong season,

try to toss their manes and hoof the ground,
but their joints have seized during the long years away.

Even twitching an ear to flick off a horsefly
is an effort. It can't be safe for them here,

a forest of wooden horses
and a hint of kerosene on the breeze.

But that horsefly – isn't it also made of wood?
Painted brown and gold, a touch of green on the eyes?

Yes, a balsa-wood horsefly, labouring into flight,
with much buzzing of its engines.

TOURISM

I saw the toppled dictator laid out in the park.
I saw apartment blocks where petunias
trailed over bullet holes in the concrete.

I knew of course to stay away from dogs
but was surprised that in the cafés
it was a crime to speak the wrong language

though in the streets they were more tolerant:
a man with a long beard recited
some guttural verses, and someone threw a coin.

There was a Museum of Griefs
with the usual rusting paraphernalia.
They gave you a lantern and sent you into the castle

to view the obscenities of wealth and the oubliettes.
You could walk it off on a beach of grit and sleet,
but the ruined watchtowers were out of bounds.

They were drawing up a guidebook,
and the tour would end on the medieval bridge
(which would be strung with coloured lights by then)

and they would re-open the restaurants,
and teach the waiters to smile,
and at night the lights would shine on the river,

and it would look a bit like the Seine,
or the Danube, or the Arno,
or the river that runs through Prague, whatever it's called.

DAMNATIO MEMORIAE

How earnestly our scholars enquire into
the toppling of the queen Hatshepsut.
She was twenty years dead after all

when they ganged in the temple with ropes
and bound her, and heaved and sweated,
and shook the walls with the noise of the felling,

when they chiselled off the nose and lips,
scratched out the eyes, hacked off the breast,
made smooth white work of her.

What starts as one thing becomes another.
Why else would they take such exquisite care
to sweep her up and shovel her into the pit?

They rendered her down into grit, and then
they walked her on the soles of their feet
into the houses where their wives were waiting.

LOST/LUST

Stumbling under the kapok tree,
fevering between its cathedral buttresses,
I am loster than lost in a place
where every known sound has its counterpart:

tap dripping into a metal bucket,
fluorescent tube about to blow,
the flicking of switches, the tuning of radios,
a tent unzipped – the jungle crawls with spies –

and I'm looking for the kind of nest you can find
if you peel back the bark, only it's the nest itself
you're tearing down: a wall, a nursery chamber –
you can't move here without a massacre.

At night I'd know it by the points of bluegreen light,
the larvae glittering in the psychedelic dark,
but by day I need a guide to tell me
this sort good to eat, this one not –

if only I'd been paying attention, not
distracted by the circus of high jinks overhead,
the thought that nothing would induce me –
still it's not for food I want these scurrying things

but for the droplet of liquid inside each one,
because the river-scent I thought I caught this morning
has been atomised by heat
and I know there's a birdcall I should follow to find it again –

but is it the hoatzin, with its smoker's cough,
or the tinamou, wet finger round the rim of a glass?
I've sweated out that wisdom and now I only
shiver and burn to wreck the nest, to put my dry mouth
to the broken place, taste panic and allspice.

UNDERGROUND

Lost here, you are precisely located.
When the torch cuts out, you hear first
the chromatics of water, tracking back
on glass feet through rock to find itself,

and next the hush of the library:
rustle of papers, scholarly scratch of the pen,
a volume slipped from a shelf and replaced.
(Records are kept of everything
as it leaves this place, or returns.)

Then your own inner sounds.
Breath, like a trapped bird
flying a corridor end-to-end.
Heart, that piece of civic effort.
Gut and gland, muscle, saliva,
synapse, enzyme, maybe even
the fidgeting of single atoms

like guests near the end of a party
thinking it must soon be time
to drain their glasses, find their coats
and take their separate ways home.

STONE AND BONE

They sit out the long afternoons together
in the forgotten parlour at the edge of the field.
Stone gives Bone the benefit of her wisdom

but Bone still mourns lost marrow and cartilage,
still dreams of articulation.
Empty now for the wind to whistle through
and the rain to trickle through
and the eye of the moon to peer right in,
all the secret sponge and coral and polymer
scooped and scraped and washed into the earth.
She is cracked and godforsaken,
disbanded and made forensic,
though once she put forth life like leaves –

Stone, chock-full of the translated dead,
all griefs traced through her from source to sea,
is past such vanities, past desire,
is no longer homesick, thinks dispassionately
of chitin, coprolite, gravity, ice.
Oh but Bone would get up and walk if she could,
get free of Stone and her homilies, the way
she sits there boring on about *the long view*,
her back warmed by the sun, and small birds
going chip, chip in their quarries among the trees.

ELDERFLOWER

Spilling your bridal whites over the churchyard wall,
slipping them off into my hand,
dusting my wrist with powder –
elixir of musk and honey, blanc de blancs –

I take you for a sign, just when I need one
along the lane, in the maze of lanes
with their dense hedges, ditches hidden under leaves,
the blind bend, the owl and the speeding van.

The rachis flushed with pink where it divides,
the panicle a host of new stars,
a few still closed in their silken nibs,
white glowing with green in the long June dusk.

Token of freshness, growing out of silence –
grant me remission, a truce with the past.
Make everything possible, here, now
in this clean state of erasure. I ask

not to start again, but to lose my way
down the steep track in the deepening dark
and to find instead this common-or-garden grace.
To break you and carry you with me as a torch.

SWIMMING POEM

*It is only irritating to think one would like to be
somewhere else. Here we are now.*

John Cage

No normal person would undress here,
this mean afternoon in early summer,

the river a brown gash in the field's fabric,
froth of petrochemicals, stink of the city's
ratty underwear strewn under the open sky.

So what am I, some kind of pervert,
some kind of puritan? Barefoot on cowshit
and bits of broken brick. Lowering myself
like a wonky ladder down a coalhole.
As if there's something fine about it.

Perhaps there is something fine about it:
throwing open all the small windows of the body,
taking your chances with the dirty world.
Listen, you heifer by the fence, aghast and drooling,

I'm not going to wait for the holy moment,
for the water to be rinsed clean in my honour.
I won't hold out till the stonefly nymph returns
or the pilgrim dips his cup and drinks again.

I'll let the sulphurous rain have my clothes,
while I steep myself in the stained and seedy present
and say *I am part of this*

ACKNOWLEDGEMENTS

Acknowledgements are due to *London Review of Books* and *Poetry Review*, where some of these poems first appeared.

I am grateful for the wisdom and encouragement of Nigel Pantling, Jacob Polley, Michael Symmons Roberts, Robin Robertson and Martha Sprackland.